HARPER

An Imprint of HarperCollins*Publishers*

First published in Great Britain 2022 by Farshore
An imprint of HarperCollins*Publishers*
1 London Bridge Street, London SE1 9GF
www.farshore.co.uk

HarperCollins *Publishers*
195 Broadway, New York, NY 10007

Written by Susie Rae
Illustrated by Ulises Farinas
Color by Gabriel Cassata

ISBN 978 0 06 313755 4
Printed in the United States of America
23 24 25 PC 10 9 8 7 6 5 4 3 2

DUNGEONS & DRAGONS

BEHOLD!

A Search and Find Adventure

KEEP YOUR EYES PEELED

'Tis I, Myopus, the All-Seeing, a beholder. Unfortunately, my many years are beginning to take their toll. My eyes aren't what they once were, which is why I need an attentive understudy to learn the ways of the watcher. Could that apprentice be you? Only time will tell. Before you begin your adventure through the Forgotten Realms, you'll need to know what to be on the lookout for. The creatures you see on the page before you will be aiding me on my quest. First point of order, introductions are necessary ...

MYOPUS THE ALL-SEEING

Your first task is to find me in each of our destinations, before turning your attention to my motley band of monsters.

BLOBERT

Just who is Blobert? It's hard to say, for I've seen him as a puddle, an ooze, and a flowing stream. He's actually a black pudding, but loves to change shapes. He'll be a tricky one to spot.

KLARICE

Kobolds might be ten-a-copper, and you'll see many of them on your travels, but Klarice is unique among her kind. She's much friendlier than her kin and always willing to lend a hand, particularly if that involves sneaking around towns and tombs ...

SNAPPY

As if one shapeshifting entity isn't enough, our little game will task you with spotting two! Snappy is a crafty and conniving mimic, capable of taking many forms. His myriad eyes and vicious teeth are often a dead giveaway though.

SILEVIN BLEAKSTIR

I know what you're thinking: we're missing someone here. But I would never make such an oversight! Silevin the invisible stalker is entirely undetectable to the untrained eye! You must seek him by looking for objects that are out of place — a floating glass, a sword wielded on its own and suchlike.

QUSTA-QOR

At first glance, you might think Qusta-Qor, with their flamboyant purple armour and skeletal visage, would be easy to spot. However, they're currently going through quite the change, from a mighty lich to a sneaky demilich. By the end of our journey, Qusta-Qor will be nothing but a floating skull. Very hard to pick out of a crowd.

Our quest will takes us on a whirlwind tour of the Forgotten Realms, to locations that are as varied as they are hectic. Keep an eye out for these boxes, which will show you some extra things to find at each town, tomb or dungeon we visit!

?	?	?	?	?

THE PARTY

You're not the only one taking your first step into a world of adventure. Indeed, we'll be treading in the wake of a brand new adventuring party as they battle, barter and become heroes along the way. With every step they take, they'll gain new gear and abilities — maybe even a familiar or two — so make sure you keep track of their level ups wherever we may go.

Naenan Granthar
Elf Ranger

Taiyo Abboz
Human Cleric

Hjalmor Stormborn
Dwarf Fighter

Scholdeg Bouldertooth
Gnome Rogue

Kellabrix
Halfling Wizard

CONTENTS

My eyes may be failing, but I still have enough power to see exactly where our adventure will take us. From the frigid north of Icewind Dale to the sweltering jungles of Chult, up and down the Sword Coast, and maybe an expedition down to the Underdark! Keep your wits about you as we set out on our quest.

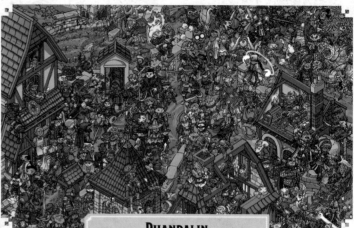
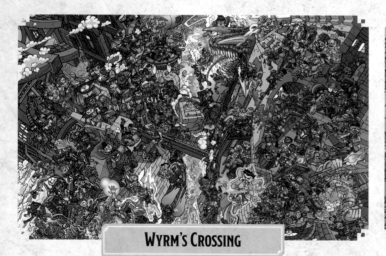
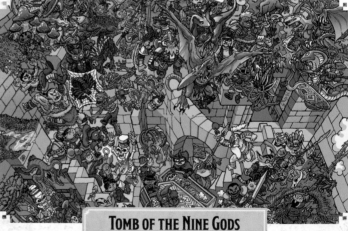

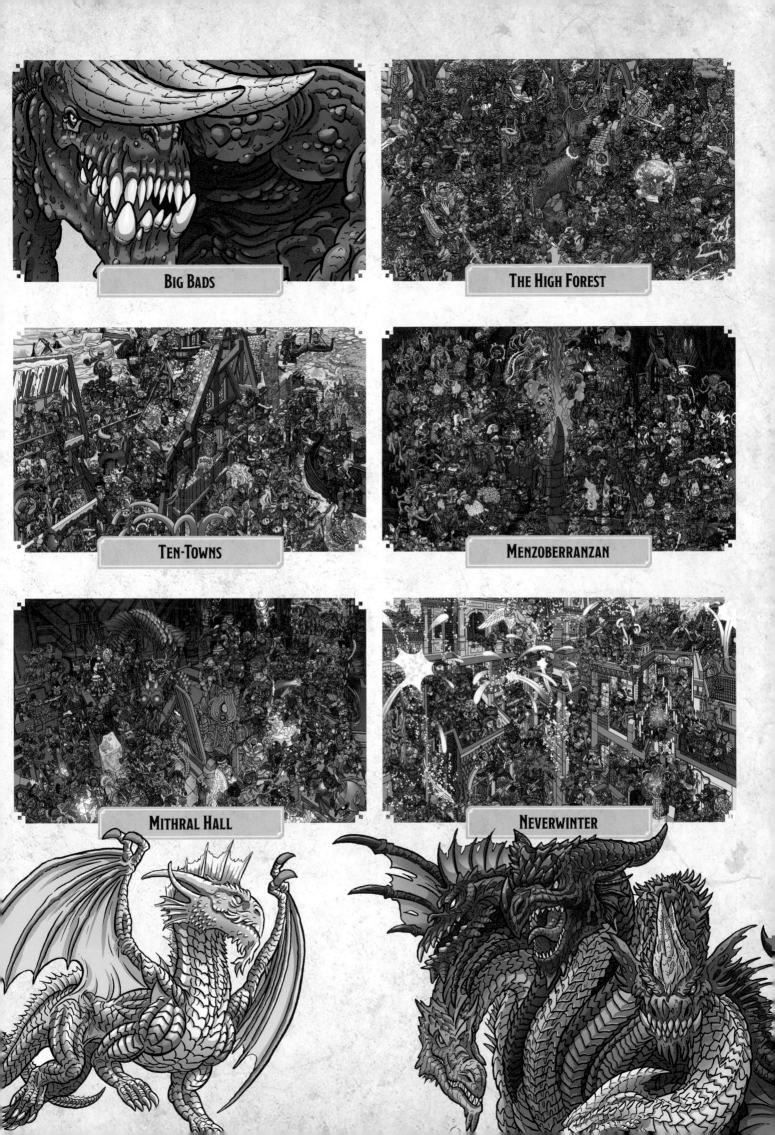

BIG BADS

THE HIGH FOREST

TEN-TOWNS

MENZOBERRANZAN

MITHRAL HALL

NEVERWINTER

THE YAWNING PORTAL

We begin our journey in the Yawning Portal, a bustling tavern in the city of Waterdeep. Popular among heroes resting up between quests or looking for their next adventure, it is famous for the deep well in the middle of the tavern, which leads into the Undermountain. Try not to fall in it just yet ...

HAG STIRRING A CAULDRON

VOLOTHAMP GEDDARM

PSEUDODRAGON

GNOLL

BUGBEAR

PHANDALIN

Our journey takes us next to the small town of Phandalin, where many adventuring parties begin their quests. This little village is home to all sorts of people, including farmers, miners and adventurers, who are preparing for a sojourn to the nearby Sword Mountains. Keep your eye out for trouble, as heroes and villains alike pass through here with regularity.

LIZARDFOLK

MINSC AND
BOO

DRAGONBORN
SCHOLAR

AWAKENED
SHRUB

DEATH DOG

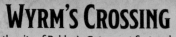

WYRM'S CROSSING

Visitors to the city of Baldur's Gate must first make their way across the daunting Wyrm's Crossing. This enormous stone bridge is built around Wyrm's Rock, a small yet imposing island that rises far above the river and connects to the metropolitan city. It's famous for being home to the legendary mercenary group known as the Flaming Fist.

| ULDER RAVENGARD | KENKU MONEYLENDER | PALADIN | WATER GENASI SEA CAPTAIN | GNOME MONK |

TOMB OF THE NINE GODS

As we venture deep into the rainforests of Chult, you will notice the ancient Tomb of the Nine Gods. Only the bravest adventurers dare to enter ... and those who do should tread carefully, lest they be greeted with a nasty surprise or two. The tomb is said to house the Soulmonger, a dark artefact created by the legendary lich Acererak.

DRAGONBAIT

DRUID CASTING A SPELL

TOMB GUARDIAN

KING OF FEATHERS

RAS NSI

LUSKAN

Welcome to the busy port town of Luskan, otherwise known as the "City of Sails". You can meet all kinds of fascinating folk here, but be careful ... that friendly sailor you're chatting to in the marketplace may turn out to be a ruthless, swashbuckling pirate!

TORTLE SAILOR   WULFGAR   KUA-TOA   SAHUAGIN   AQUATIC ELF RANGER

THERE BE DRAGONS!

Every explorer in the Forgotten Realms has heard tales of dragons: powerful, ancient creatures who spend centuries guarding their treasure hoards. For more advanced monster experts, such as yourself, here's a field guide to the types of dragons you might encounter.

METALLIC DRAGONS

These dragons are easily recognised by their bright, shiny scales. Often followers of the dragon god of justice, Bahamut, metallic dragons are known for being wise, reclusive creatures who will only fight as a last resort. But be careful ... if you get on the wrong side of a gold dragon, it may be the last thing you do!

CHROMATIC DRAGONS

Chromatic dragons come in all different colours – blue, green, red, white, black – and are intelligent and fearsome combatants. Those who follow Tiamat, Queen of Evil Dragons, revel in destroying or dominating smaller creatures.

FAERIE DRAGONS AND PSEUDODRAGONS

Dragons also have many smaller relatives, including faerie dragons and pseudodragons. Tiny, playful pseudodragons are often kept as pets or familiars. Mischievous faerie dragons can expel powerful euphoria gas as a weapon if threatened. One key difference between the two is that faerie dragons can talk, while pseudodragons can only communicate using telepathy.

DRAGONBORN

Descended from dragons, dragonborn take on a humanoid form. They have the same scaly skin, sharp claws and breath weapons as dragons, but are much smaller, live shorter lives, and walk around on two legs, like a human.

WYRMLING

Like most creatures, dragons start out as babies – in their case their first form is the wyrmling. It might be young, but its breath attack is still super deadly.

DRACOLICHES

What happens when you cross a dragon with the undead? Well, you get something you'd probably rather not meet in a dark cave! Dracoliches were once dragons, but used powerful necromancy to gain near-immortality, preserving their souls in a magic vessel.

Big Bads

When you've been around as long as I have, you get to know all about the creatures of the Forgotten Realms, from the weird and wonderful to the utterly terrifying. Luckily for you, brave adventurer, I'm here to warn you about the monsters that you really need to look out for ...

Pit Fiend

The Infernal Plane, known as the Nine Hells, is home to legions of devils. Some of the most powerful infernal creatures are pit fiends, who rule over the Nine Hells and revel in the pain and suffering of others.

The Tarrasque

There is no creature more terrifying than the tarrasque. An enormous lizard with deadly teeth, spines, claws, horns, and an unquenchable thirst for destruction, the tarrasque can and will obliterate everything in its path. It cannot be killed, and is imprisoned at the core of the world, in a deep, magical sleep. I only hope it doesn't wake up in my lifetime ...

SZASS TAM

As a red wizard, the lich Szass Tam ruled the kingdom of Thay in the Forgotten Realms. He was often diplomatic but prone to fly into rages that spelt the end for his victims. He cared only for power, however, and he spent most of his unending life warring with and deposing the fellow leaders of Thay, known as the Zulkir.

LICH

Sometimes, a spellcaster will get too hungry for power, craving magical knowledge beyond what is possible to gain in a single lifetime. These mages use dark necromancy to turn themselves into liches, undead beings who warp their souls in exchange for immortality. The only way to kill a lich is to find and destroy the vessel that contains the remains of the creature's twisted soul.

VECNA

Beginning life as a human wizard, Vecna rose to power with the aid of his lieutenant, Kas. However, Kas ultimately betrayed him and destroyed his physical form. All that remained were a hand and an eye, which are now highly sought-after magical items. Vecna's spirit remained intact, however, and the worship of his dedicated followers elevated him to the status of a demigod.

ROC

Keep an eye out on the skies, because you don't want to be caught unawares by one of these enormous birds. Don't underestimate how absolutely, utterly enormous rocs are – with a wingspan of almost 200 feet, they are known to hunt elephants and even whales. They're not necessarily aggressive towards humanoids, but if you come across a bad-tempered roc, you might be in trouble!

THE HIGH FOREST

Much of what exists among the dense trees of the High Forest is a mystery known to very few. If you look closely, you'll discover all manner of magical creatures – most of them friendly – or spot one of the elven communities who call the forest their home.

AARAKOCRA PALADIN

UTHGARDT BARBARIAN

ELF RANGER

FIRBOLG RANGER

EARTH GENASI

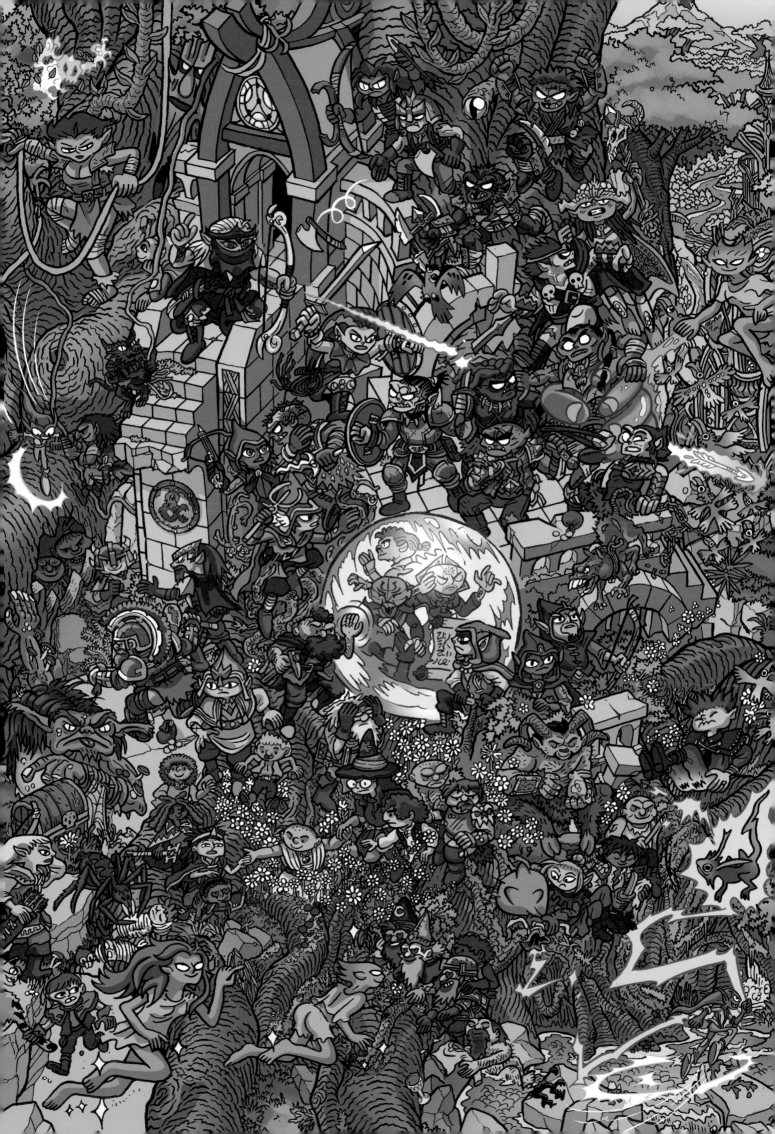

TEN-TOWNS

Next, let's travel to the frozen wastelands of Icewind Dale. The weather in Ten-Towns is harsh, so only the hardiest of folks choose to live here. Among those who call the tundra home are barbarian tribes, as well as those who want to live away from the searching eyes of civilisation. I wonder what they're trying to hide ... maybe we'll find out!

GOLIATH BARBARIAN

JARLAXLE

CRAG CAT

SNOWY OWLBEAR

ORC FISHERMAN

MENZOBERRANZAN

Welcome to the area that I once called home, the Underdark, which is a cavernous labyrinth beneath the world's surface. The bustling cavern city of Menzoberranzan is the stronghold of the worshipers of Lolth, the dread Spider Queen.

DRIDER   UMBER HULK   DROW WITH A DRAGON EGG   TIEFLING ROGUE

MIND FLAYER WITH A RAT

MITHRAL HALL

Say what you like about dwarves, but they know their rocks. Carved into the bedrock of the Frost Hills, Mithral Hall has been a mine, a fortress and a dwarven town over the centuries. Veins of a valuable metal called mithral run through the walls – if you're very lucky, you might be able to use your keen eye to get rich around here!

| CATTI-BRIE | SORCERER | YUAN-TI BARD | NIGHTMARE | GITHYANKI WARRIOR |

NEVERWINTER

Neverwinter is known as the "Jewel of the North", and for good reason! Despite being in the far north of Faerûn, the river that runs through this beautiful, vibrant city is heated by a fire primordial, giving it a lovely, warm climate year-round.

FIRE-WORSHIPERS

HALF-ORC FLOWER SELLER

ELVEN ROGUE

RAKSHASA

DICE CRAFTER

ANSWERS

And with that, our adventure is at an end. But how well did you fare? Let's revisit the stops on our quest to see if you spotted everything.

THE YAWNING PORTAL

1. Klarice
2. Blobert
3. Snappy
4. Qusta-Qor
5. Silevin Bleakstir
6. Myopus
7. Hag stirring a cauldron
8. Volothamp Geddarm
9. Pseudodragon
10. Gnoll
11. Bugbear
12. The Party

PHANDALIN

1. Klarice
2. Blobert
3. Snappy
4. Qusta-Qor
5. Silevin Bleakstir
6. Myopus
7. Lizardfolk
8. Minsc and Boo
9. Dragonborn scholar
10. Awakened shrub
11. Death dog
12. The Party

THE HIGH FOREST

1. Klarice
2. Blobert
3. Snappy
4. Qusta-Qor
5. Silevin Bleakstir
6. Myopus
7. Aarakocra paladin
8. Uthgardt barbarian
9. Elf ranger
10. Firbolg ranger
11. Earth genasi
12. The Party

MENZOBERRANZAN

1. Klarice
2. Blobert
3. Snappy
4. Qusta-Qor
5. Silevin Bleakstir
6. Myopus
7. Drider
8. Umber hulk
9. Drow with a gold dragon egg
10. Tiefling rogue
11. Mind flayer with a rat
12. The Party

NEVERWINTER

1. Klarice
2. Blobert
3. Snappy
4. Qusta-Qor
5. Silevin Bleakstir
6. Myopus
7. Fire-worshipers
8. Half-orc flower seller
9. Elven rogue
10. Rakshasa
11. Dice crafter
12. The Party

MORE THINGS TO FIND

So you made it this far, eh? Then you're ready for some extra training. I may have spotted a few things on our journey that are of particular interest. If you're inclined to prove yourself even further, then retread your footsteps and find all of these extra elements.

THE YAWNING PORTAL

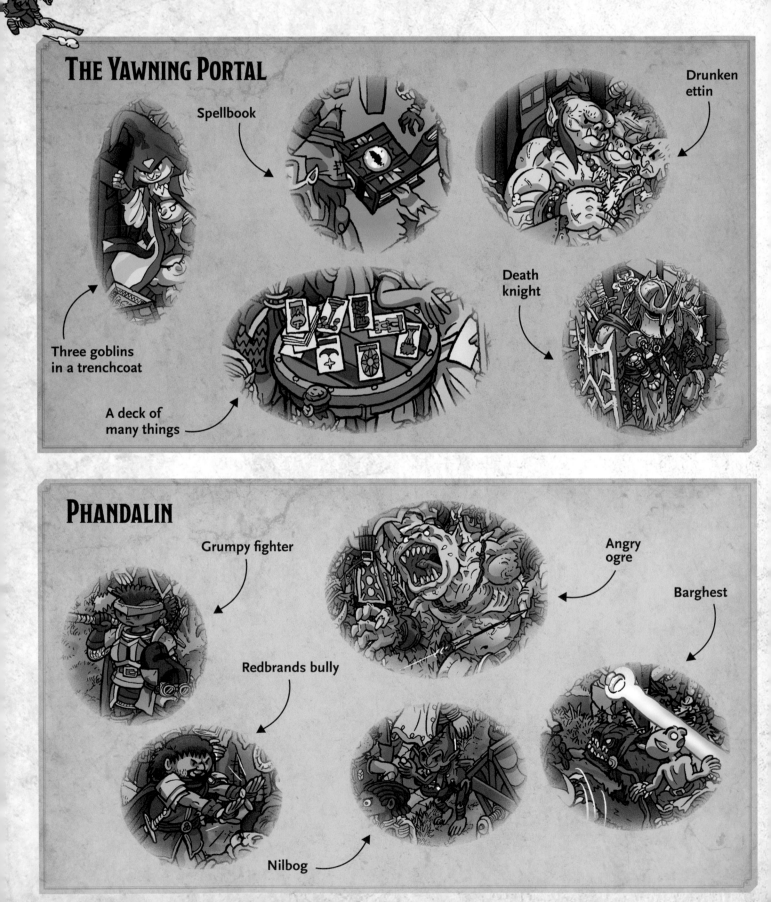

Spellbook

Drunken ettin

Death knight

Three goblins in a trenchcoat

A deck of many things

PHANDALIN

Grumpy fighter

Angry ogre

Barghest

Redbrands bully

Nilbog

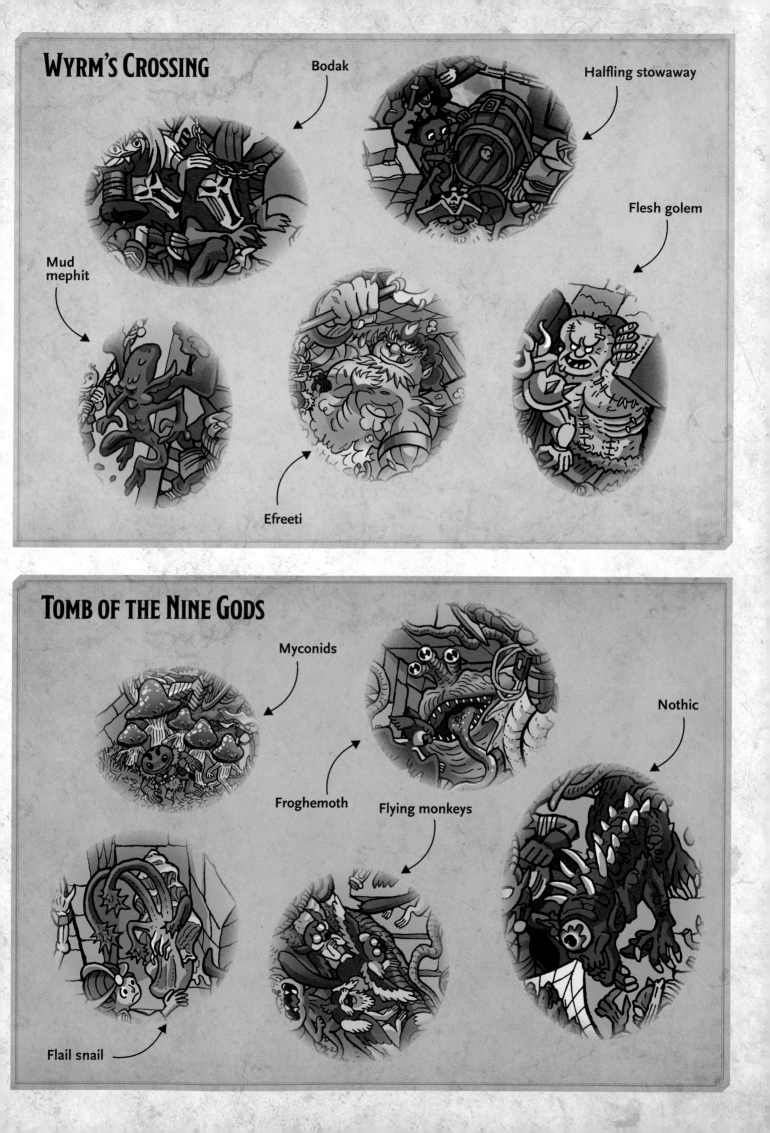

WYRM'S CROSSING

Bodak

Halfling stowaway

Flesh golem

Mud mephit

Efreeti

TOMB OF THE NINE GODS

Myconids

Nothic

Froghemoth

Flying monkeys

Flail snail

Luskan

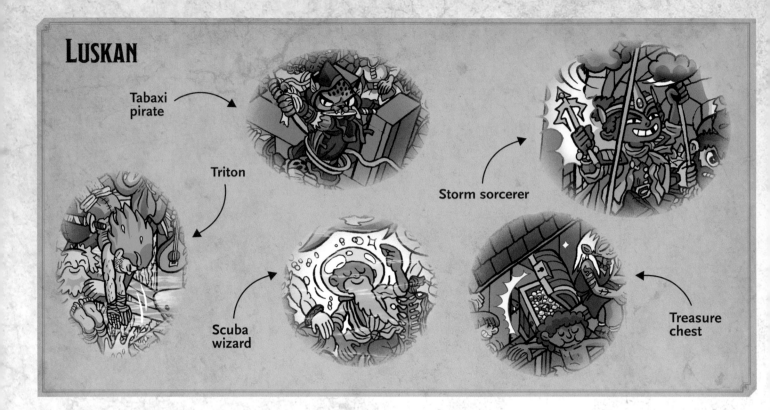

- Tabaxi pirate
- Triton
- Storm sorcerer
- Scuba wizard
- Treasure chest

The High Forest

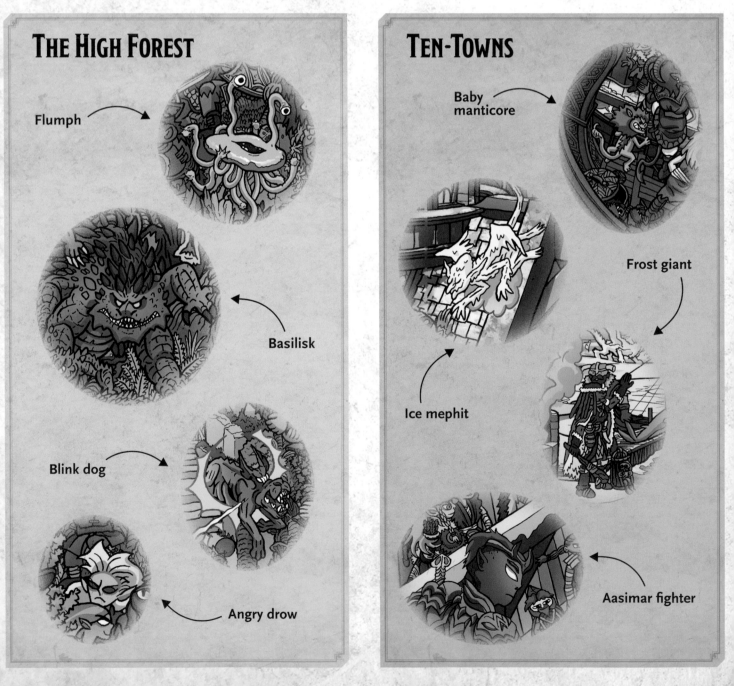

- Flumph
- Basilisk
- Blink dog
- Angry drow

Ten-Towns

- Baby manticore
- Frost giant
- Ice mephit
- Aasimar fighter

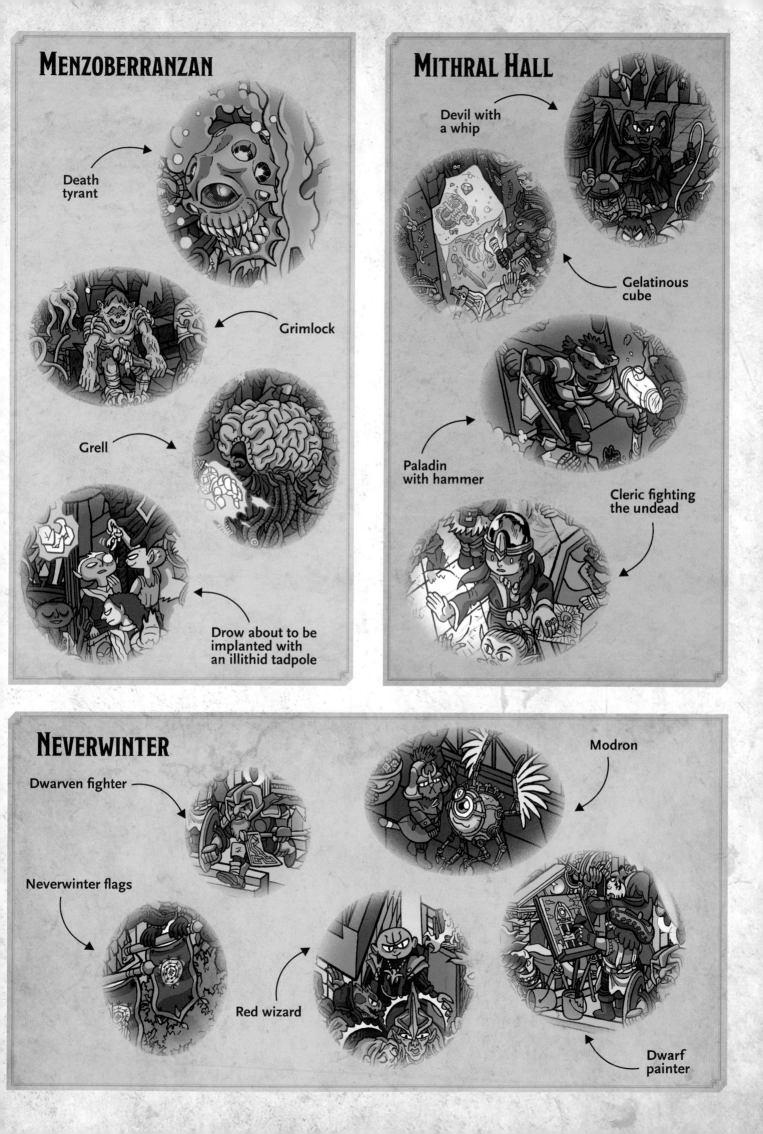

Menzoberranzan

Death tyrant

Grimlock

Grell

Drow about to be implanted with an illithid tadpole

Mithral Hall

Devil with a whip

Gelatinous cube

Paladin with hammer

Cleric fighting the undead

Neverwinter

Dwarven fighter

Neverwinter flags

Modron

Red wizard

Dwarf painter

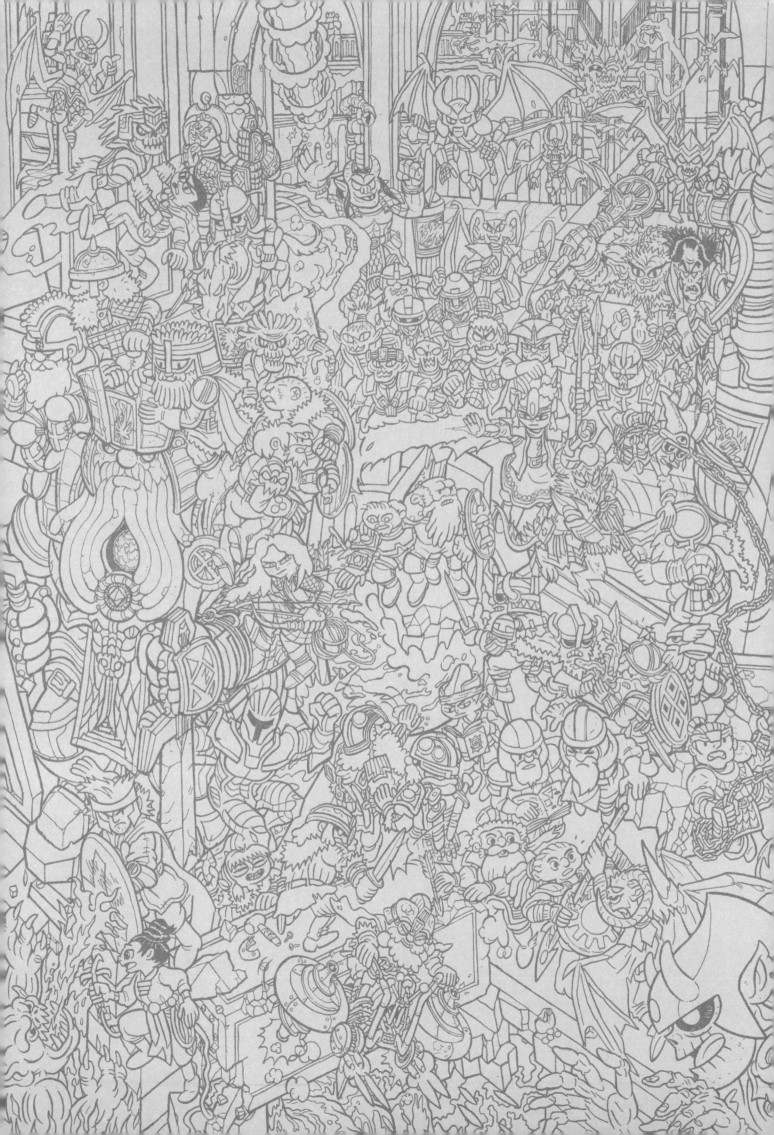